Welsh Soups & Savouries

recipes from the traditional
heart of Welsh cookery,
including
cawl – Wales'
meal-in-a-bowl
by

Bobby Freeman

If you were to ask the average non-Welsh person which is the national dish of Wales, they would reply vaguely: 'Welsh Cakes?' or perhaps 'Welsh Rarebit'?

The truth is that it is neither of these. But Welsh people themselves are unlikely to mention the dish which I think really is Wales' national dish, partly because they have never considered it in such terms, partly because they would not expect you to comprehend it.

Its name in Welsh is *cawl* – but if you look the word up in the dictionary you will simply get 'broth or soup'. But *cawl*, in the sense I am describing, means a complete meal… of chunks of meat and root vegetables, potatoes and leeks, redolent of herbs and with a distinctive flavour of its own despite its similarity in its combination of ingredients to other soups/stews/meals in a pot common to the cookery of the western world.

People tasting *cawl* for the first time are instantly captivated; even sophisticated palates succumb: I once heard a group of film-makers in Wales exclaim, 'This is *soul* food!'

And so it is. On a cold winter's day, there is nothing like it. It's a dish which touches our inherent yearning for the primitive comfort of simple, sustaining food.

But *cawl* has other meanings. To the expatriate Welshman it is home, the hearth and everything he loves and yearns for of his roots in Wales.

It also has its darker side. To those who lived through the hard times in rural Wales it is emotive in a different way, for it represents monotony and poverty which they do not want to recall. *Cawl*, day after day, and poor, thin *cawl*, too, as often as not for breakfast, dinner and supper, is no proud memory, nor does it inspire any sense of promotion to outsiders as a 'national dish'. Best forgotten.

And there is a fourth meaning, a derogatory one, nothing to do with food, to denote a hotchpotch – of ideas, or affairs, or whatever.

Lastly – you only have to watch the sea streaming into Porthcawl on the Glamorgan coast to realise why they called it 'a broth of a bay'.

Despite its less fortunate associations, *cawl* is still made regularly in Wales today, and is becoming increasingly popular for informal public get-togethers as an expression of nationalism.

Because the pot-over-the-fire tradition was so strong in Wales, and lasted so long, many of the recipes in this little book are dishes of that kind – easy to make, flavoursome and nourishing, economical in their use of fuel. There are a few charming surprises – the Glamorgan sausages which vegetarians have discovered, the salt duck – astonishingly good – and the next oldest dish of all (for *cawl* I think must be the very oldest) – Welsh rarebit, which modern technology is enabling to be made in its original form.

3

Cawl

The basic dish of meat, root vegetables, potatoes and leeks, and sometimes cabbage, finds many variations, nor is it made exactly the same in two kitchens together. Like any other 'national' dish it has regional variations, and in north Wales it tends to be called *lobscows* from the English 'sheep broth'.

Cawl is traditionally eaten in wooden bowls with hand-carved wooden spoons which vary in design from region to region. There were also pretty, flowered pottery *cawl* bowls. Bread and cheese are taken with the *cawl* to make an extremely satisfying meal.

But in times of hardship the broth would be drunk first, on its own. Then the meat eaten with some potatoes. Next day, root vegetables would be cooked in the leftover broth, still rich with nourishment. This was known as *cawl twymo* (second *cawl*), or *cawl ail-dwym* (re-heated *cawl*). Otherwise, the meat would be taken out when cooked, the vegetables added to the broth, and when this was served in bowls everyone helped themselves to the meat from a large wooden platter in the centre of the table.

Basic Instructions:

Precise quantities are unimportant, so these are just a guide. For a weight of 900g / 2 lbs of meat – about 2 large parsnips, 3 large carrots, 1 small swede turnip, 2 medium onions, 2 or 3 leeks and 675g / 1½ lbs of potatoes (the tiny, marble-size new potatoes are most prized). You will need a big pan to hold all this, covered with cold water, so reduce quantities by half if you only want 3–4 servings. Flavour with plenty of thyme or Winter savory, parsley, bay leaf and 1 or 2 cloves, and I like to add celery. Season with whole black peppercorns (leave the salt to add later). Some cooks thicken the *cawl* with a handful of oatmeal or flour and water paste.

I leave the leeks out of the cooking altogether and sprinkle them on top of the bowls of *cawl*, chopped very fine, with plenty of freshly-chopped parsley, so they are crisp, crunchy and peppery. If you do cook them, don't add them until the final 10 minutes of cooking time. The same applies to cabbage, if you include it.

Cook the tougher meats for an hour or so first before adding the vegetables, which should be cut up roughly (not finely) to ensure the character of the dish. And brown both meat, onions and vegetables first in a little oil or dripping.

Variations on the Basic Theme:

Bacon & Brisket: this is my favourite combination and most will agree it is the best – the brisket gives the *cawl* a very particular quality and taste. A hock-end of bacon – smoked for preference – pairs well with an equal weight of brisket. Make sure everyone gets a portion of both in their bowl. Since *cawl* is in fact better re-heated, you can lift the surplus fat off the top next day when it is cold.

Bacon only: very fatty home-cured bacon was traditionally used (plenty of 'stars' on its face) but nowadays our tastes and lifestyles are for something leaner. Again a hock-end is useful, or shoulder bacon, or you can be extravagant and use a piece of gammon or other lean cut.

Lamb & Shin: again the addition of beef improves the flavour – shin of course will require substantial pre-cooking.

Quick *cawl*: for this version everything – meat and vegetables – is cut up small and cooks relatively quickly. The result is more stew-like than true *cawl*, and not so good. This version was almost always thickened with flour and water and therefore looked whitish. A direct descendent is:

'Magimix' *cawl*: inevitably, the ease with which the food processor chops the vegetables to small dice is irresistible to cooks who have made more brews of real *cawl* in a kitchen where running water was a luxury than city-spoiled seekers after tradition like myself care to think about – and who can blame them? It's not proper *cawl*, though!

Leek & Potato Soup
Cawl Cennin

450g / 1 lb peeled potatoes
450g / 1 lb leek (incl. the tender green)
1.8l / 3 pints water or chicken stock
1 dessertspoon salt

Slice or dice the potatoes, slice the leeks thinly, discarding the tough green end parts. Simmer together 40–50 minutes (or pressure cook – NB: this soup doesn't work too well in the microwave). Mash the vegetables or liquidise. Check seasoning and reheat.

Exact quantities are not important for this soup, which is a marvellous base for the addition of leftover or fresh vegetables. If you use chicken stock and increase the seasoning and stir in up to 300ml / ½ pint of cream when it cools before finally chilling it, *cawl cennin* becomes *Vichyssoise* – a chef's extension of the simple country soup he or she remembered from his or her mother's kitchen while working far away in Vichy… *Potage Bonne Femme* as it is called in France.

Hare Broth
Cawl Coch Ysgyfarnog

1 hare
1 medium swede or turnip
6 leeks
450g / 1 lb potatoes
oatmeal, parsley, salt

An alternative to jugging or casseroling hare, which tempers the strong flavour somewhat. In the old days in Wales hare *cawl* was a tremendous feast. Soak the skinned and cleaned hare in cold, salted water overnight. Cut into joints and place in a large pan with enough water to cover, plus about 1.2l / 2 pints. Add the turnip, chopped small. Bring to the boil, simmer for 30 minutes, then add parsley, finely-chopped leeks, plus the salt. After another 30 minutes mix the oatmeal to a paste with cold water and add. Continue cooking until the hare meat drops off the bone. Remove and keep warm. Now add the potatoes, cut small, and boil until cooked. Traditionally the hare meat was served separately on wooden plates and the broth and vegetables in a bowl.

Michaelmas Goose
Gŵydd Mihangel

Another feast of the old days, given by the farmer to his tenants when they paid their rents. After the harvest the geese were turned on to the fields to glean them: they fattened quickly. Goosefeather beds helped keep out the winter cold in Welsh hill-farm bedrooms; some of the bigger feathers were used in the kitchen – the large wing pinion for sweeping the hearth, the smaller wing feathers for brushing flour or oatmeal while baking.

To make this *cawl* the prepared goose was boiled in plenty of water, with a bowlful of chopped onions and thickened with oatmeal. The thick, fatty broth which resulted would be just what was needed to keep out the cold... but not today!

Curiously, there is a Russian way with goose which is similar in that it is cooked in a pot with finely-chopped onions – but no water at all. In this case there is no fat as the goose is first skinned and the fat pulled off with the skin. The bird is then cut into eight pieces which are placed on a bed of onions, previously sweated until pink, seasoned with pepper and salt, in a heavy pan, tightly covered and placed over the lowest possible heat. In about an hour a liquor will have formed; in six hours the meat will be done and sitting in several pints of delicious gravy. Add 1 tablespoon of redcurrant jelly, pile the meat on to mashed potato or buckwheat and pour the gravy over.

Broad Bean Broth
Cawl Ffa

900 g / 2 lbs piece of bacon
225g / ½ lb broad beans (shelled)
450g / 1 lb potatoes
small swede or turnip
2 leeks
parsley, pinch sage

Soak the bacon overnight in cold water, then cover with
fresh cold water, bring to the boil and skim. Simmer
about 1 hour. Add the potatoes and turnip, cut roughly,
and when these are nearly done, the beans. Thicken with
a paste of 1 tablespoon of oatmeal and water if liked, and
sprinkle finely-chopped leeks and parsley on the top
to serve.

Brandy Broth
Cawl Mawr

In *How Green Was My Valley* Richard Llewellyn refers to
'Brandy Broth' as a dish similar to this (only in his case it
was a fully-stuffed chicken, a piece of lean lamb and a
piece of ham, with a 'noggin of brandy' – three in all –
slipped in every 15 minutes in the later stages of cooking,
and with the first a pint of home-brewed ale. Sounds
superb!).

700–900 g / 1½–2 lbs lean meat or bacon
900g / 2 lbs chicken
225g / ½ lb carrots
450g / 1 lb leeks
225g / ½ lb parsnips
small swede or turnip
parsley, salt and pepper

Make as for basic *cawl*, simmering 2½–3 hours, adding
the chopped leeks and parsley at the end. Serve the
broth as the first course, the chicken and meat garnished
with the vegetables as the second course, with the
remaining liquor thickened as gravy, with separately
boiled potatoes or *stwns rwdan* (see p.18).

Market Pie

Katt Pies

As there is no 'k' in the Welsh alphabet, this name is a tremendous puzzle, although the pies were indeed associated with Templeton Fair (12 November) in Pembrokeshire. Explanations on lines of 'pussy pies' are not allowed!

Mutton pies like these, spiced and sweetened with sugar and dried fruits (originally made thus to disguise the taste of tainted meat) were long favourites with the British, and widely sold at fairs and markets.

450g / 1 lb flour
175g / 6 oz suet or lard
150ml / ¼ pint milk & water
good pinch salt
225g / ½ lb minced mutton or lamb
225g / ½ lb currants
225g / ½ lb brown sugar
salt & pepper

Make a hot water crust by melting the fat in boiling milk and water – pour liquid into a well of flour and mix with a wooden spoon until cool enough to handle, then shape to pies 4 inches in diameter. Arrange filling in layers – meat, fruit, sugar, seasoning as you go. Cover with a round of pastry. Bake for 30 minutes in a hot oven (425ºF, Gas 7, 220ºC). Eat hot.

Faggots
Ffagoden

Commercially-made faggots are one thing, domestic versions another. The former usually contain the lights, melt and heart to stretch the liver (which is now relatively expensive). In traditional domestic recipes liver only is used, but in this one, given to me by a north Pembrokeshire friend, it is combined with belly pork and the result is especially good.

Note: Faggots are unknown in the US, where the word means a rather unsavoury tramp.

900g / 2 lbs belly pork
450g / 1 lb pig's liver
700g / 1½ lbs breadcrumbs
700g / 1½ lbs onions or shallots
good pinch sage, salt & pepper
pig's caul (shawl)

Mince the two meats and the onions, mix with crumbs and seasonings. Divide into 50g / 2 oz balls and wrap each in a 5-inch square of caul. This is the lacy, fatty substance covering the foetus: it is now difficult to obtain even from butchers, so if you can't get any, roll the faggots in a little flour. Place them in rows in a baking tin. Pour over stock to come well up the faggots and bake for 2 hours in a low oven (240°–310°F, Gas ¼–2, 115°–155°C), adding more boiling water if necessary to keep the faggots nearly covered.

Glamorgan Sausages
Selsigen Morgannwg

'The breakfast was delicious, consisting of excellent tea, buttered toast and Glamorgan sausages, which I really think are not a whit inferior to those of Epping.'
George Borrow, *Wild Wales*.

In George Borrow's day there were many sausages of this type, dipped in egg-white and rolled in crumbs rather than encased in skins. It is reasonable to suppose that these took their name from the Glamorgan cheese used for them – it was an especially hard, white cheese made from the milk of Glamorgan cattle, an almost extinct breed now re-introduced to Wales. The sausages are nicer than you might think, freeze well and are popular with vegetarians. Eat them with a sharp and spicy sauce, like tomato.

150g / 5 oz white or brown breadcrumbs
75g / 3 oz grated hard cheese
1 small onion
1 egg
pinch dry mustard
pinch mixed herbs
25g / 1 oz butter
pepper and salt

Mince or chop the onion very fine and soften in the butter before adding to the other dry ingredients – it makes shaping the sausages easier. Separate the egg and bind the mixture with the yolk. Divide into 6 small sausage shapes, moulding with your hands, then roll in flour, dip into the lightly-beaten egg white and finally roll in fine breadcrumbs. Deep fry in hot oil until the coating is nice and crisp. Do not re-heat in a microwave.

Green Pancakes
Crempog Las

Another good vegetarian dish or an alternative to bread
or potatoes as an accompaniment to meat or bacon; in
fact, it quite likely originated as a meat-stretcher in lean
times. It requires some skill to make as the batter must
be stiff enough to support the onions and allow them to
cook through.

225g / ½ lb flour
2 eggs
chopped parsley
spring onions or shallots
milk to mix (300ml / ½ pint approx.)
pepper and salt

Make a batter with the flour, eggs and milk. Stir in the
parsley and onion and seasoning. Cook on both sides as
for pancakes, but over a very moderate heat in a well-
buttered, heavy pan. Make sure they are cooked right
through. Spread with butter and eat hot.

Rabbit Pie
Pastai Gwningen

This nice old recipe announces its age by the seasoning of nutmeg and the addition of beefsteak and ham – one that possibly found its way from a *plas* to a well-to-do farm kitchen.

1 rabbit
225g / ½ lb beefsteak
125g / ¼ lb cooked ham
stock
shortcrust or puff pastry
2 teaspoon chopped parsley
nutmeg, pepper and salt

Soak the rabbit in cold, salted water for a few hours. Joint and place in a pie dish with the ham and steak cut into small pieces. Sprinkle with the parsley and seasonings, add enough stock to just cover and put a pastry lid on top. Bake in a very moderate oven (320°–370°F, Gas 3–4, 160°–190°C) for 1½ hours, covering the pastry with paper or foil if it becomes too brown.

Sweet Lamb Pie
(18th century)

This is a 'gentry' and earlier version of 'Katt Pie', with remnants of medieval cookery in the throwaway suggestion to include hardboiled eggs, sweetmeats and citron (lemon). As with all these very old recipes, quantities are not given, hence their appeal to cooks with an experimental bent. Use lean and tender lamb – 900g / 2 lbs will give you a good, family-sized pie for 4/5. The recipe comes from the MS recipe book from Gogerddan mansion, near Aberystwyth.

> Cut your Lamb in pieces and season it with cinnamon, mace, nuttmeg, and salt, sugar a little, then put it into your pie with butter and reisins of the sun [big raisins], bake it: then melt some butter and beat 2 yolks of eggs with a little sack [sweet sherry] and sugar, then put your melted butter to it*, and when your pie comes out of the oven put in your cawdle, you may put in hard eggs, sweet meats and citron if you please.

> * the cawdle

I would take the option not to include the last items. This is well worth trying.

Mashed Turnips with Liver

Stwns Rwdan a Iau

A *stwns* or mash of turnips and potatoes, well peppered and salted and with a good knob of butter worked in, is a surprisingly good dish on a cold winter's day. In north Wales it was frequently combined with a dish of liver and onions, made as follows:

450g / 1 lb liver
2 medium onions
flour
fat for frying
300ml / ½ pint stock

Roll slices of liver in seasoned flour and then brown in hot fat. Remove to a casserole. Chop onion fairly fine and fry until golden brown. Put with the liver. Shake a little flour into the pan, adding more fat if necessary and scraping up all the nice brown tasty bits from around the pan. Carefully brown the flour, then add stock to make a good gravy. Pour over the liver and onions and cook in a moderate oven (320º–370ºF, Gas 3–4, 160º–190ºC) until the liver is tender (about 45 minutes).

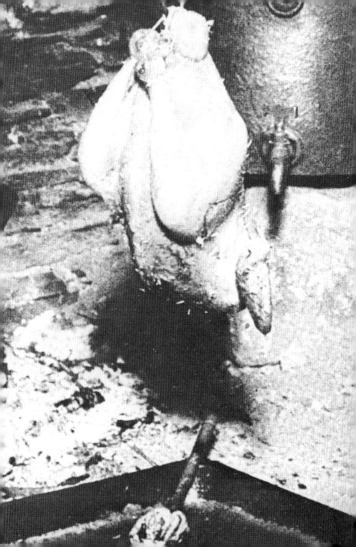

Chicken & Leek Pie
Pastai Cyw Iâr a Cennin

This is an adaptation of Lady Llanover's instructions for the 'Hermit's Chicken and Leek Pie' in *Good Cookery from Wales* (1867). The Hermit, incidentally, was simply the central character in the book who expounded all her culinary theories. She does not say where the recipe originates, but I do not think it is particularly Welsh in origin, despite the leeks. I would guess she is working from a quite old recipe from an early cookery book, as there are discernable shades of early 17th-century dishes in the recipe.

a boiling fowl
3 or 4 slices of cold tongue
a bunch of small leeks
a large onion
1 stick celery
mixed herbs, parsley, salt
3 tablespoons cream
175g / 6 oz flour, 85g / 3 oz shortening for the pastry

(Lady Llanover's specified mutton fat, another clue to the age of the recipe.)

Cover the chicken with water in a large pan, bring to the boil and skim. Then add the onion, quartered, celery and herbs and seasoning. Simmer 1½–2 hours until the bird is tender. Remove from the pan and strain the stock into a basin. Chill to a jelly, remove fat from the top. Clean and cut the leeks into 1 inch lengths. Divide the chicken into joints and lay in a pie dish with the slices of tongue and the leeks and finely-chopped parsley. Moisten with some of the chicken jelly. Cover with shortcrust, leaving a small opening in the centre (cut a piece of pastry into a fancy shape and bake alongside the pie to use later to cover the hole). Bake in a hot oven (410°–440°F, Gas 6–7, 210°–230°C) until the pastry is a light golden brown. Pour warmed cream through the hole in the top, then cover. Serve warm. To serve cold, omit the cream.

Salt Duck
Hwyad Hallt

Another recipe from *Good Cookery from Wales*, but this one I think is in the Welsh tradition, at least in the eastern border areas. Lady Llanover specifies a 3-day salting and I think it is worth the extra day from the 1 or 2 days given in less meticulous recipes. There is also no question about the advantage in taste and texture from the very gentle simmering achieved by the use of a *bain-marie* for this dish (Lady Llanover called it a 'double', i.e. the duck in one pan of water inside another filled with water). This is a delicious way of cooking duck and little understood. One of its virtues is that all the fat is carried off in the water, leaving only lean, tender, delicately-salted meat. Use the stock for lentil soup. You may have to use a frozen duck if nothing else is available: I do not think this is the calamity some people would have it.

Salt duck can be eaten hot or cold. If hot, try it with the onion sauce below, also from *Good Cookery from Wales*. Cold, it is good with green salad, or an orange and watercress salad.

Onion Sauce: Cut up 4 onions and stew in a 'double' with a little water until tender, pour off the water, mix it with 15g / ½ oz flour, add 300ml / ½ pint milk, stir till smooth. Press through a wire sieve (or liquidise), return to the double saucepan, stir well while heating through.

Onion Cake
Teisen Nionod

This was one of my best discoveries for giving a meal a distinctive Welsh flavour. It has its cousin in the *pommes de terre à la boulangère* of France, but in Wales the dish was made in a cake tin (possibly for want of an alternative) and thus assumed the name 'cake'. I use a thick earthenware round or oval oven dish, and a fairly firm, waxy potato which will hold its shape in the slices.

900g / 2 lbs potatoes
1 or 2 onions
butter
pepper & salt
300ml / ½ pint beef stock (optional)

Butter the inside of a thick baking dish generously. Peel and thinly slice the potatoes and soak them for a few minutes to draw out the starch. Drain and dry in a clean cloth.

Cover the bottom of the dish with a thick layer of potatoes, then a layer of finely-chopped onions, season, and dot with butter. Continue until the dish is full, finishing with potatoes and dotting the top with extra butter. Add good beef stock if using. Cover with greaseproof paper or foil and bake in a hot oven (410°–440°F, Gas 6–7, 210°–230°C) for about an hour, when the potatoes should be soft and cooked right through. Ten minutes before the end of cooking time remove the cover to brown and crisp the top.

Welsh Chicken
Ffowlyn Cymreig

Another dish reminiscent of a very old recipe – 'chicken stewed with lettuce and bacon' (for lettuce, read cabbage). The use of the word *ffowlyn* suggests a boiling fowl.

1 chicken
225g / ½ lb bacon
225g / ½ lb carrots
2 large leeks
a small cabbage
300ml / ½ pint stock
butter
bouquet garni
pepper and salt
25g / 1 oz butter + 25g / 1 oz flour

Truss the chicken. Cut the bacon and carrots into small pieces and fry in butter until they are just turning colour. Place the chicken on top with the leeks, herbs and seasoning. Pour round the stock, dot the chicken with a little butter, cover and simmer for 2–3 hours. Cook the cabbage separately and make a bed of it on which to serve the chicken and the other vegetables. Boil up the liquor and thicken with the flour and butter worked together and pour around or serve separately.

Parsley Pie
Pastai Persli

One tends to wonder about this recipe: why the sugar in the custardy filling? I'm inclined to think it is a carry-over of an old idea from the times when sugar went into almost everything, before the distinction between sweet and savoury seasoning took place. The idea persists in sugar-baked ham.

2 eggs
300ml / ½ pint milk
1 dessertspoon flour
2 tablespoons sugar
1 dessertspoon chopped parsley
40g / 1½ oz fat bacon
salt and pepper
shortcrust pastry

Line a deep pie dish with the pastry. Mix the flour with a little of the milk, beat the eggs with the rest of the milk, add to the blended milk and flour with the salt, sugar and parsley. Lay the bacon cut in small dice in the pie, pour the custard over, bake in a fairly hot oven (380°–400°F, Gas 5, 195°–205°C) for 30 minutes or until the mixture has nicely set and cooked through. The same pie can be made with leeks instead of parsley.

Mum's Supper
Swper Mam

Variations on the bacon theme are endless in Welsh cookery. No wonder, with a pig in every back yard! This quickly-made dish is comforting on a cold winter's night – which is perhaps how it got its name.

8 bacon or ham rashers
2 onions, finely chopped
125g / 4 oz grated cheese
pepper and salt

Layer bacon, onion and cheese in a shallow, ovenproof dish, seasoning each layer and ending with a layer of bacon. Bake in a hot oven (410º–440ºF, Gas 6–7, 210º–230ºC) for 30 minutes or until the top bacon is crisp. Good with jacket potatoes.

The Miser's Feast
Ffest y Cybydd

This was originally an expedient for getting two meals out of one – the potatoes mashed in the nourishing liquor one day, the bacon with a fresh boiling of potatoes the next… hence the name. The idea is similar to that of a 2-day *cawl*.

There is something innately satisfying about the combination of bacon and potatoes, especially when the potatoes are nice and mealy.

potatoes
slices of bacon or ham
onion
salt and pepper

Cover the bottom of a heavy saucepan with whole, peeled potatoes and a sliced onion. Cover with water and a little salt, and pepper, and a lid, and bring to the boil. Now put the ham or bacon slices on top of the onion and potatoes, replace the lid and simmer slowly until the potatoes are cooked through and most of the water absorbed.

Honeyed Welsh Lamb
Oen Cymreig Melog

By fair means or foul, this recipe has crept into 'traditional' Welsh cookery. I have been quite unable to trace any Welsh origin and I am certain no cottager would contrive such a dish. Perhaps from a *plas*? Nothing appears in any of the MS collections from Welsh nations, although it has some connections with late medieval cookery.

Nevertheless, it is a good dish and is featured most successfully at the *Hwyrnos*, or 'Welsh Night', suppers in Swansea as an alternative to *cawl*.

1.4–1.8kg / 3–4 lb leg or shoulder of Welsh lamb*
300ml / ½ pint cider
225g / 8 oz Welsh honey
2 tablespoons rosemary
1 teaspoon ginger
salt and pepper

*Welsh lambs are smaller than other breeds, thus being nearer the bone the meat is sweeter.

Rub the joint with salt, pepper and ginger and leave for 30 minutes or so to absorb. Double-line an ovenproof dish with foil (this is most important as burnt honey is impossible to remove). Place the joint on the foil, spread the honey over the meat, sprinkle with rosemary. Pour cider all around. Roast for 30 minutes in a hot oven (410°–440°F, Gas 6–7, 210°–230°C) then lower heat to moderate (320°–370°F, Gas 3–4, 160°–190°C) for a further hour. You can cover the joint for the first half of the cooking time if you wish, otherwise baste at intervals, adding more cider if necessary to avoid the honey catching. Garnish with long sprigs of rosemary.

Gower Oyster Soup
Cawl Wystrys Gŵyr

Another recipe which does not belong to the true
tradition of Welsh cookery but which was doubtless
associated with the houses of the wealthy and the hotels
of Mumbles and Gower west of Swansea in Victorian
times, when the oyster fishing industry of Oystermouth
was at its height. The recipe in Welsh collections is
traceable to Mrs Beeton.

6 dozen prepared oysters
2.4l / 4 pints mutton broth
50g / 2 oz butter
40g / 1½ oz flour
300ml / ½ pint cream
salt, cayenne, mace

Season the stock and bring to the boil. Meanwhile, work
the butter and flour together to a paste (*beurre manié*)
and add to the broth in small pieces, stirring briskly to
thicken. Simmer for 5 minutes. Pour over the oysters, re-
heat but do not boil. Stir in the heated cream (or milk if
the soup is wanted less rich).

Laverbread for Breakfast
Bara lawr i Frecwast

If you are lucky you will be offered 'laverbread' with your breakfast bacon when you are staying in Wales, especially in south-west Wales. 'Laverbread' is a bit of a misnomer, for it is seaweed, not bread. But a literal translation of the Welsh is *lawr* – laver, *bara* – bread; however, in this case bread is meant in the sense of sustenance. To avoid confusion I try to call it laverweed or simply laver. It's a thin, transparent variety found on the west coast of Wales. It takes a lot of boiling to make it edible and in its prepared form it is sold on the cheese, bacon or fish stalls in local markets. Mixed with medium oatmeal and made into little patties and fried in bacon fat, it is a most enduring feature of Welsh home cooking.

But laverweed can be used in other ways, too.

Soup: 2 tablespoons of laver stirred into 575ml / 1 pint of good vegetable soup with a chicken or mutton stock, then liquidised to an interesting green colour. Serve with a swirl of cream and croutons. Not traditional in any way.
Sauce: Two ways –
1) laver added to a Béchamel sauce to serve with roast lamb or grilled lamb chops.
2) Laver and orange juice mixed with good gravy from roast lamb and served with it. Astonishingly good.
Salad: Dress laver with a few drops of olive oil and lemon juice and a good grind of black pepper. Serve with fingers of dry toast, like caviare, which in appearance it resembles. Welsh caviare? Wickedly, that's what I once menu-dubbed it … *'Caviare Cymreig'*.

Roasted Cheese
Caws Pobi

This is the true 'Welsh Rarebit' as far as the Welsh are concerned. They were inordinately fond of it from the earliest times in its simple form: later it developed into one of the many regional 'rarebits' or 'rabbits' as a cheese sauce on toast.

The original was simply a piece of hard cheese roasted, or toasted, on one side only, before the fire, on a piece of barley or other wholegrain bread. Now, with the microwave, we can take a gigantic backward leap across the centuries, for nothing makes *caws pobi* more correctly and faster than a few seconds in the microwave.

Also in the series:
A Book of Welsh Country Cakes and Buns
A Book of Welsh Bread
A Book of Welsh Country Puddings and Pies
A Book of Welsh Fish
A Book of Welsh Bakestone Cookery

Also by Bobby Freeman:
Lloyd George's Favourite Dishes (1974, 1976, 1978 – Ed.)
Gwent – A Guide to South East Wales (1980)
First Catch Your Peacock: The Classic Guide to Welsh Food
(1980)
Welsh Country House Cookery (1983)
Welsh Country Cookery – Traditional Recipes from the
Country Kitchens of Wales (1987)

First impression: 1987

© Bobby Freeman 1987

ISBN: 978-1-78461-890-2

Published and printed in Wales on paper from well-maintained
forests by Y Lolfa Cyf., Talybont, Ceredigion SY24 5HE
e-mail ylolfa@ylolfa.com
website www.ylolfa.com
tel 01970 832 304
fax 832 782